D0579341

This Place I Know

POEMS OF COMFORT

This Place I Know

POEMS OF COMFORT

Poems Selected by Georgia Heard

illustrations by
Eighteen Renowned Picture Book Artists

CANDLEWICK PRESS
CAMBRIDGE, MASSACHUSETTS

Contents

A Note from the Anthologist

During any difficult time, we all need a place where, as Faiz Ahmed Faiz writes in his poem "Song," "the heart [can] rest." Poetry has always offered comfort and consolation during sorrowful times, and reminded us of the places in our lives, inside and out, that can help us heal.

Although the original impetus for this anthology was to comfort children in the aftermath of 9/11, I believe these poems resonate even now. Children are still coping with the trauma of 9/11 and its aftermath, as well as many other personal and global tragedies. The world has changed, and we are all so much more aware of the toll these tragedies have taken—whether through terrorism, war, or natural disaster.

As I read through poems for inclusion in this anthology, I kept asking myself one question: What words can comfort? I tried to choose poems that touch upon feelings of fear and loss, remind us that we are not alone in despair, and assure us that dreams can be born even from ruin.

Several poems focus on the enduring greatness of cities, including Ann Turner's beautiful poem about New York City, "The Beginning." Cities like New York, London, Madrid, Banda Aceh, Niamey, and New Orleans have endured devastating circumstances in recent years. They are a symbol of hope as we witness the courage and tenacity of people who persevere in the face of tremendous fear and adversity.

My hope is that these beautiful and powerful poems and images will help children all over the world as Gwendolyn Brooks proclaims in "A Little Girl's Poem"—continue "to live," "to laugh," and "to sing."

Georgia Heard

THIS PLACE

There is this place I know
where children go to find
their deepest feelings
they look behind the trees
for hiding wants and angers
bashful joys
this place is quiet
no shouts may enter
no rolling laughter
but only silent tears
to carry the feelings
forward in waves
that wash the children
whole

Eloise Greenfield

Holly Meade

STARS

I like the way they looked down from the sky
And didn't seem to mind the way I cried.

And didn't say, "Now wipe away those tears,"
Or, "Tell us, tell us what's the matter here!"

But shining through the dark they calmly stayed,
And gently held me in their quiet way.

I felt them watching over me, each one—
And let me cry and cry till I was done.

Deborah Chandra

Yumi Heo

HOLD FAST YOUR DREAMS

Within your heart
Keep one still, secret spot
Where dreams may go,
And sheltered so,
May thrive and grow—
Where doubt and fear are not.
Oh, keep a place apart
Within your heart,
For little dreams to go.

Louise Driscoll

Hiroe Nakata

LULLABY

Will you hold me in your lap?
Will you cuddle me so tight?
Will you kiss my fearful brow,
And not turn off the light?

Will you soothe away my worry?
Will you sing the sweetest song?
Will you chase my fears away,
And rock me all night long?

Georgia Heard

Vivienne Flesher

A LITTLE GIRL'S POEM

Life is for me and is shining!
Inside me I
Feel stars and sun and bells singing.

There are children in the world
all around me and beyond me —
here, and beyond the big waters;
here, and in countries peculiar to me
but not peculiar to themselves.

I want the children to live and to laugh.
I want them to sit with their mothers
    and fathers
and have happy cocoa together.

I do not want
fire screaming up to the sky.
I do not want
families killed in their doorways.

Life is for us, for the children.
Life is for mothers and fathers,
life is for the tall girls and boys
in the high school on Henderson Street,
is for the people in Afrikan tents,

the people in English cathedrals,
the people in Indian courtyards;
the people in cottages all over the world.

Life is for us, and is shining.
We have a right to sing.

Gwendolyn Brooks

Giselle Potter

TROUBLE, FLY

Trouble, fly
out of our house.
We left the window
open for you.

Fly like smoke from a chimney.
Fly like the whistle from a train.
Fly far, far
away from my family,
mumbling in their sleep.

Trouble, fly.
Let our night
be a night of peace.

Susan Marie Swanson

Elisa Kleven

TO YOU

I think I could walk
through the simmering sand
if I held your hand.
I think I could swim
the skin shivering sea
if you would accompany me.
And run on ragged, windy heights,
climb rugged rocks
and walk on air:

I think I could do anything at all,
if you were there.

Karla Kuskin

William Steig

COMMITMENT IN A CITY

On the street we two pass.
I do not know you.
I did not see
if you are—
fat/thin,
dark/fair,
young/old.

If we should pass again
within the hour,
I would not know it.
Yet—
I am committed to
love you.

You are part of my city,
my universe, my being.
If you were not here
to pass me by,
a piece would be missing
from my jigsaw-puzzle day.

Margaret Tsuda

Jill McElmurry

HOLES

Strangest of gaps
their goneness —
mother, father, loved friends

the black holes
of the astronomer
are not more mysterious

this kind of hole
will not be filled
with candle flames
or even a thousand thoughts

the hole is inside us
it brims over
is empty and full at once.

Lillian Morrison

Shane W. Evans

STRENGTHEN THE THINGS THAT REMAIN

Rainbows still live in the sky and green grass
is growing everywhere. Clouds have familiar shapes
and sunsets have not changed color in a long time. Thunder
still follows lightning and spring comes after winter's
misery.

A tree is still a tree and a rock is still a rock. A warbler
sings its familiar song and coyotes howl
in disconcerting harmony. Grasshoppers still hop

to their own music,
bees still buzz with excitement, and squirrels
still jump like acrobats. Mountains still contain mystery
and oceans surge with eternity. Bears still sleep in winter

and eagles fly higher than other birds. Snakes have an affinity
for the ground, while fish
are content in water. Patterns persist,
life goes on, whatever rises will converge.

Do what you will, but strengthen the things that remain.

Nancy Wood

Petra Mathers

Life is mostly froth and bubble,
Two things stand like stone;
Kindness in another's trouble,
Courage in your own.

—A. L. Gordon—

Laura McGee Kvasnosky

SONG

Pain will cease, do not grieve, do not grieve—
Friends will return, the heart will rest, do not grieve, do not
grieve—
The wound will be made whole, do not grieve, do not grieve—
Day will come forth, do not grieve, do not grieve—
The cloud will open, night will decline, do not grieve, do not
grieve—
The seasons will change, do not grieve, do not grieve.

Faiz Ahmed Faiz

Vladimir Radunsky

DREAMS

Hold fast to dreams
For if dreams die
Life is a broken-winged bird
That cannot fly.

Hold fast to dreams
For when dreams go
Life is a barren field
Frozen with snow.

Langston Hughes

Matt Tavares

FROM SONG OF THE BROAD-AXE

What do you think endures?
Do you think a great city endures?
Or a teeming manufacturing state? or a prepared constitution? or
        the best built steamships?
Or hotels of granite and iron? or any chef-d'oeuvres of engineering,
        forts, armaments?

Away! these are not to be cherish'd for themselves,
They fill their hour, the dancers dance, the musicians play for
        them,
The show passes, all does well enough of course,
All does very well till one flash of defiance.

A great city is that which has the greatest men and women,
If it be a few ragged huts it is still the greatest city in the whole
        world.

Walt Whitman

Peter Sís

RING AROUND THE WORLD

Ring around the world
Taking hands together
All across the temperate
And the torrid weather.
Past the royal palm-trees
By the ocean sand
Make a ring around the world
Taking each other's hand;
In the valleys, on the hill,
Over the prairie spaces,
There's a ring around the world
Made of children's friendly faces.

Annette Wynne

Melissa Sweet

"Hope" is the thing with feathers—
That perches in the soul—
And sings the tune without the words—
And never stops—at all—

And sweetest—in the Gale—is heard—
And sore must be the storm—
That could abash the little Bird
That kept so many warm—

I've heard it in the chillest land—
And on the strangest Sea—
Yet, never, in Extremity,
It asked a crumb—of Me.

Emily Dickinson

G. Brian Karas

THE PEACE OF WILD THINGS

When despair for the world grows in me
and I wake in the night at the least sound
in fear of what my life and children's lives may be,
I go and lie down where the wood drake
rests in his beauty on the water, and the great heron feeds.
I come into the peace of wild things
who do not tax their lives with forethought
of grief. I come into the presence of still water.
And I feel above me the day-blind stars
waiting with their light. For a time
I rest in the grace of the world, and am free.

Wendell Berry

Kevin Hawkes

THE BEGINNING

This is where it begins
like God really lives in New York
and he opens his hands, PRESTO!
there are subway trains
  churning through the dark,
and Brooklyn Bridge swaying
  all its lights like ribbons,
and buildings climbing the sky
  the clouds just near,
and sea lapping the docks
  where men bellow and yell.
And there are children in parks
  always on swings,
and dogs running underfoot
  like bits of escaped rug,
and museums full of bones, birds,
  paintings and teeth—
long ago and here and always
  He said,
"Here's New York!"

Ann Turner

Chris Raschka

About the Illustrators

Shane W. Evans

"My inspiration for creating this artwork came to me in thinking about the events of September 11 and the poem 'Holes' by Lillian Morrison. Like the person in my illustration, I often find myself using my hands to frame little sections of the world, creating an instant composition, a 'portable window' to look through. 'Holes' inspired in me the representation of something no longer there. I was in New York City during and after the tragedy and remember looking into the sky; the composition had changed completely and dramatically. It was daunting to put up my 'portable window' and not see something otherwise so familiar."

Vivienne Flesher

"As I was working on my piece for this book, I couldn't feel anything. I think I was numb from it all. But after I was done, I felt grateful to be able to join with these other fine artists in an attempt to help all those affected by the terrible events of September 11."

Kevin Hawkes

"Wendell Berry's poem 'The Peace of Wild Things' spoke very strongly to me. As a young man, whenever I felt sad or lonely, I went hiking in the woods or mountains. There is something very comforting, even magical, about walking slowly out of doors, trying to spot wildlife, or sitting quietly in tall grass, looking at the insects. Smelling the earth and hearing the sounds of nature are powerful reminders that life is good."

Yumi Heo

"Often, after September 11, I've found myself looking up at the night sky. The stars twinkle as usual, as they did a million years ago, as they did on September 11, and as they will tomorrow. Though something tremendous and sad has changed us all, I am comforted by the beauty of the night sky."

G. Brian Karas

G. Brian Karas has taken on many subjects in the books he has written and illustrated for children. This wide range represents his interest in portraying the humorous, frightened, adventurous, painful, brave, and tender moments that are childhood. Perhaps the most difficult for the artist was his contribution to this anthology. He says, "I wondered how an artist could provide comfort for the world's universal grieving for the tragic events of September 11, or any tragic event for that matter, with words or pictures. But I found that it was words and pictures that most comforted me during difficult times and maybe I could possibly help with my art. My hope is that it *will* — somewhere, to someone."

Elisa Kleven

"'Trouble, Fly,' by Susan Marie Swanson, resonates with me, as the narrator puts into words what I feel each night when I put my children to bed — my hope that 'this night,' and all future nights, will be peaceful for them and for all the innocent life that inhabits our gorgeous, one and only world." Elisa Kleven is the illustrator of many picture books, among them, *Abuela* by Arthur Dorros, *Our Big Home* by Linda Glaser, and her own *The Paper Princess, Sun Bread,* and *The Dancing Deer and the Foolish Hunter.* She lives in Albany, California, with her husband, daughter, son, and various pets.

Laura McGee Kvasnosky

"'Life is mostly froth and bubble,' by A. L. Gordon, is a simple poem that aligns kindness and courage. Reading it, I remembered a dream my sister and I shared when we were six and eight. We dreamed we were awakened by a gossamer lady and a huge lion sitting on our cedar chest. Although this was frightening, we both knew the lady was kind. To create the image for this poem, I folded the folktale of Androcles and the Lion into the dream."

Petra Mathers

"When I first read 'my' poem, 'Strengthen the Things That Remain' by Nancy Wood, I panicked. So much nature, all this harmony. Where was the peril? Where were the buildings? Then, one day, I noticed the shell that sits on my windowsill. It looked like the poem, like a monument to the things that remain."

Jill McElmurry

"As I read the poem 'Commitment in a City,' I thought of what I love best about city life: watching everyone, so different yet so close together, sharing an avenue, a sidewalk, or a patch of grass, doing the dances that city people do with or around each other as if they were choreographed. I've lived in coastal towns and mountain towns, in wide-open desert places and narrow, jungly canyons, but living in cities has taught me what it means to be human."

Holly Meade

"Finding a place to weep and wash your troubles away — what lovely images Eloise Greenfield's words bring to mind in 'This Place.' Perhaps some comfort can be found here, in the place where images and words come together."

Hiroe Nakata

"I was born in Japan and grew up there. Now I live in New York. On a quiet night, the moon makes me feel at home, no matter where I am. When I was little, the moonlight that came through my bedroom window brought many dreams to my sleepy head."

Giselle Potter

"I drew a lot as a child because that is what everyone around me did. Both my grandparents were painters and my grandfather always invited other people to add to his paintings." Giselle Potter's first illustration job was a drawing for the *New Yorker*. Her first children's book was *Mr. Semolina-Semolinus: A Greek Folktale;* she has illustrated eleven other children's books since then. Giselle Potter lives in New York's Hudson Valley.

Vladimir Radunsky

Vladimir Radunsky was born in Russia and has lived in New York City since 1982. He has illustrated many books for children, among them *The Maestro Plays* by Bill Martin Jr; *Yucka Drucka Droni* by Eugenia Radunsky; *An Edward Lear Alphabet,* in collaboration with Bagram Ibatoulline; *Discovery* by Joseph Brodsky; *Square Triangle Round Skinny; Table Manners,* which he co-wrote and co-illustrated with Chris Raschka; and *Howdi Do, Bling Blang,* and *My Dolly,* all written by Woody Guthrie.

Chris Raschka

"This beautiful poem, 'The Beginning' by Ann Turner, sent me to a beautiful spot I know, the middle of the Manhattan Bridge. There, with the trains to and from Brooklyn running by, I painted this picture of the southern tip of Manhattan, with the Brooklyn Bridge and the towers of Wall Street and even a glimpse of the Statue of Liberty — all bits of this place I know and love."

Peter Sís

Peter Sís is the author and illustrator of numerous award-winning books for children. He has lived in downtown Manhattan for almost twenty years with his wife and two children, though he says, "I continue to be amazed by the city of New York — every day I wake up to a new dream of a new world."

William Steig

William Steig is a renowned *New Yorker* artist and the creator of numerous picture books and novels, including *Sylvester and the Magic Pebble, The Amazing Bone, Dominic, Abel's Island, Doctor DeSoto,* and *Shrek!* Of his inspiration for his illustration in *This Place I Know,* William Steig says, "I remembered Kasha and Pearl, two good old canine friends."

Melissa Sweet

Melissa Sweet has illustrated many books for children, including the Pinky and Rex series by James Howe, *On Christmas Day in the Morning: A Traditional Carol* by John Langstaff, and *Girls Think of Everything: Stories of Ingenious Inventions by Women* by Catherine Thimmesh. An amateur astronomer, she finds a lot of comfort in the night sky and is currently building a Newtonian telescope. She lives with her family in Rockport, Maine.

Matt Tavares

"When I first read 'Dreams' by Langston Hughes, I thought of how the events of September 11, 2001, left many people feeling like the broken-winged bird mentioned in the poem. In my illustration, I wanted to show the joy that can come from holding fast to our dreams, and not allowing ourselves to be paralyzed by fear and negativity."

Acknowledgments

"This Place" from *Under the Sunday Tree* by Eloise Greenfield. Text copyright © 1988 by Eloise Greenfield. Used by permission of HarperCollins Publishers.

"Stars" from *Balloons and Other Poems* by Deborah Chandra. Copyright © 1990 by Deborah Chandra. Reprinted by permission of Farrar, Straus and Giroux, LLC.

"Lullaby" by Georgia Heard. Copyright © 2001 by Georgia Heard. Reprinted by permission of the author.

"A Little Girl's Poem" from *Very Young Poets* by Gwendolyn Brooks. Copyright © 1983 by the David Company, Chicago.

"Trouble, Fly" from *Getting Used to the Dark* by Susan Marie Swanson. Text copyright © 1997 by Susan Marie Swanson. Reprinted by permission of DK Publishing Inc.

"To You" by Karla Kuskin. Copyright © 1987 by Karla Kuskin. Reprinted by permission of S©ott Treimel NY.

"Commitment in a City" from *Cry Love Aloud* by Margaret Tsuda. Copyright © 1972 by Margaret Tsuda. Reprinted by permission of the author. First published in *The Christian Science Monitor*.

"Holes" from *Overheard in a Bubble Chamber and Other Science Poems* by Lillian Morrison. Copyright © 1981 by Lillian Morrison. Used by permission of Marian Reiner for the author.

"Strengthen the Things That Remain" from *Sacred Fire* by Nancy Wood, illustrated by Frank Howell. Copyright © 1998 by Nancy Wood. Used by permission of Random House Children's Books, a division of Random House, Inc.

"Life is mostly froth and bubble" by A. L. Gordon from *Poems for Life*. Published by Arcade Publishing.

"Song" by Faiz Ahmed Faiz from *Poems for Life*. Published by Arcade Publishing.

"Dreams" from *The Collected Poems of Langston Hughes* by Langston Hughes. Copyright © 1994 by The Estate of Langston Hughes. Used by permission of Alfred A. Knopf, a division of Random House, Inc.

"What do you think endures?" from "Song of the Broad-Axe" in *Leaves of Grass* by Walt Whitman.

"Ring Around the World" from *All Through the Year* by Annette Wynne. Copyright 1932 by Annette Wynne. Used by permission of HarperCollins Publishers.

"'Hope' is the Thing with Feathers" from *The Poems of Emily Dickinson*, Thomas H. Johnson, ed., Cambridge, MA: The Belknap Press of Harvard University Press. Copyright © 1951, 1955, 1979 by the President and Fellows of Harvard College. Reprinted by permission of the publishers and the Trustees of Amherst College.

"The Peace of Wild Things" from *The Selected Poems of Wendell Berry* by Wendell Berry. Copyright © 1998 by Wendell Berry. Reprinted by permission of Counterpoint, a member of the Perseus Books Group.

"The Beginning" from *Street Talk* by Ann Turner. Text copyright © 1986 by Ann Turner. Reprinted by permission of Houghton Mifflin Company and Curtis Brown Ltd. All rights reserved.

While every effort has been made to obtain permission to reprint copyright material, there may be cases where we have been unable to trace a copyright holder. The publisher will be happy to correct any omission in future printings.

For my mother and father,
with love
G. H.

Special thanks to Shelley Harwayne, Superintendent of District 2 in Manhattan, who gave me the chance to be of service after September 11 by asking me to find poems of comfort for the New York City schoolchildren; Kara LaReau, my editor at Candlewick Press, who helped create a wider vision for this important project; and Dermot and Leo, who give me comfort every day.

First edition in this format 2006

Library of Congress Cataloging-in-Publication Data

This place I know : poems of comfort / selected by Georgia Heard ;
illustrations by eighteen renowned picture book artists. —1st ed.
p. cm.
ISBN 0-7636-1924-1 (original hardcover)

1. Children's poetry, American. I. Heard, Georgia.
PS586.3 .G74 2002
811.008'09282—dc21 2002017503
ISBN 0-7636-2875-1 (unjacketed hardcover)
2 4 6 8 10 9 7 5 3 1
Printed in the United States of America
This book was typeset in Stempel Schneidler. The illustrations were done in various media.

Candlewick Press
2067 Massachusetts Avenue
Cambridge, Massachusetts 02140

visit us at www.candlewick.com